CLIMIE , D.

HIGH SPIRITS

Sketches from

HIGH SPIRITS

and Other Revues

SAMUEL FRENCH

LONDON

NEW YORK SYDNEY TORONTO HOLLYWOOD

Fee for each and every performance by amateurs in the British Isles of any of the sketches in this volume	Code A

ISBN 0 573 07010 5

Printed in Great Britain from stereos
by W & J Mackay & Co Ltd, Chatham

CONTENTS

WATCH YOUR LANGUAGE

by David Climie

Performed in *High Spirits*

Characters

THE TRANSLATOR	*Cyril Ritchard*
MISS HUGGINS	*Thelma Ruby*
HER GENTLEMAN FRIEND	*Leslie Crowther*
THE STRONG ARM OF THE LAW	*Maxwell Coker*

The curtains open and reveal the TRANSLATOR, *an earnest gentleman in spectacles and dinner-jacket standing down* R. *There is a chair* C.

TRANSLATOR. Ladies and gentlemen, you are, of course familiar with the method of learning languages by listening to colloquial conversation on gramophone records. One language, however, has been unaccountably neglected by the record companies; I refer to American. Tonight we hope to redress this by bringing you your first lesson in colloquial Transatlantic language; or, as *they* call it—Bingo. . . . All right, Miss Huggins.

(MISS HUGGINS, *a brassy blonde, enters and strolls across to the chair, singing harshly*)

MISS HUGGINS. Ma baby's done left me!
Ma baby's done left me!

TRANSLATOR. Miss Huggins is singing a typical American folk song in which she describes how she has been deserted by her infant child.

(*There is a knock on the door off stage*)

MISS HUGGINS (*yelling*) O.K.—push it!
TRANSLATOR. Do come in.

(*A ratty* GANGSTER *enters* L)

GANGSTER. Lissen—you Hophead Sal Huggins?
TRANSLATOR. Miss Huggins, I presume?
MISS HUGGINS. So what? You got a beef comin'?
TRANSLATOR. Have you received your meat allocation?
GANGSTER (*looking round*) Gee, what a crummy joint.
TRANSLATOR. I am not *satisfied* with my meat allocation.
MISS HUGGINS. Ah, button up, you rat.
TRANSLATOR. Adjust your clothing, you rascal.

GANGSTER. Lissen—I'm movin' in on your rackets.

TRANSLATOR. I should like to join your tennis club.

GANGSTER. So how's about a slice for me?

TRANSLATOR. I would welcome some cake.

MISS HUGGINS. Listen—Sadie Steiner and me does the split.

TRANSLATOR. Miss Steiner and myself are acrobatic dancers.

GANGSTER. Steiner? That dame's a broad.

TRANSLATOR. That lady has left the country.

MISS HUGGINS. Yeah—but she's always on the level.

TRANSLATOR. She is invariably horizontal.

GANGSTER. Look—I want thoity g's.

TRANSLATOR. I require thirty horses.

MISS HUGGINS. No dice. I already got two bums to support.

TRANSLATOR (*after a horrified moment of thought*) The lady has an unfortunate affliction.

GANGSTER. O.K.—you're goin' to the chair, if I can fix it.

TRANSLATOR. I'll find you a seat—if possible.

MISS HUGGINS. Yeah? You asked for it and you're gettin' it.

TRANSLATOR. Here is your request.

(MISS HUGGINS *produces a gun and shoots the gangster twice*)

(*Making a gesture*) Bang bang.

(*As he makes the gesture* MISS HUGGINS *slips the gun into his hand. The* GANGSTER *slumps to the floor.*
     A POLICEMAN *enters* L)

POLICEMAN. O.K., lady—looks like I'm goin' to have to pinch you.

TRANSLATOR. Excuse me, madam, I am about to take a liberty.

MISS HUGGINS. Why don't you pinch him? He's got the rod.

TRANSLATOR. He has the fishing tackle—oh, you mean *me*?

POLICEMAN (*hustling the* TRANSLATOR *off*) Yeah, she means you—and she's right. Come on, Buster.

MISS HUGGINS (*leaning on the chair and nonchalantly watching them go; singing*) Ma baby's done left me . . .

TRANSLATOR. *What* was that?

MISS HUGGINS (*singing*) Ma baby's done left me . . .

TRANSLATOR. Your baby! Good heavens—Mother!

BLACK-OUT

LOST IN THE FOREST OF ELIZABETH ARDEN

Performed in *High Spirits*

Lyric by
Peter Myers & Alec Grahame

Music by
John Pritchett

BEAUTY PARLOUR ASSISTANT   *Diana Churchill*

A BEAUTY PARLOUR ASSISTANT *is contemplating her victim.*

Can I help Modom? A refill for your lipstick?
Certainly, Modom, the colour chart is on that wall.
Well, if Modom thinks that colour is attractive,
Very well, Modom—but, Modom, is that all?

It's a pity Modom's skin is so neglected,
I've a feeling several little cells have died.
Modom might increase her charm
With our Number Thirty Balm,
And revive the little corpses if she tried.
Do these blemishes disfigure Modom often?
I've an ointment that can fill those creases too,
Made from aromatic pines,
We've some interesting lines,
And, if I might say so, Modom, so have you!

May I ask, is Modom shiny by intention?
Yes, *their* cold cream may be splendid, Modom, *but* . . .
Though it's true those little pores
Should open up their doors,
Well, afterwards they really should be shut!
Modom's eyes, if Modom wished, could seem much larger,
Why not remove that film with "Sultan's Bliss"?
And a pack or two of mud
Might pasteurize your blood,
And Modom, we must watch for two of this. (*She pats her chin*)

It's a shame that Modom's hair has lost its lustre.
Home Perm? Ah, Modom, that accounts for that.
Here's a tint that you might try . . .
No, Modom, we never say dye,
Well, if Modom feels that way—perhaps a hat.
Quel dommage that Modom's eyebrows join together,

3

I fear we have a little surplus hair
May I recommend this razor?
Such a dainty stubble chaser
And of course, Modom, it can be used elsewhere.

What a pity Modom's bust has lost its tension.
Modom hasn't had ten children—how absurd!
For as I live and breathe
Those deceivers don't deceive
And really, Modom, Gay is not the word.
Has Modom ever thought about a toothbrush?
This paste tints Modom's gums Tahiti Red.
Modom now has just one part
To be garnished by our art.
Modom—may I recommend . . . (*She turns and obviously the cus-*
tomer has fainted) Oh! Modom's *dead*!

BEAUTIFUL FAMILY PORTRAIT

Performed in *High Spirits*

Words by
Peter Myers & Alec Grahame

Music by
Ronald Cass

Characters

THE DUKE	*Ronnie Stevens*
THE DUCHESS	*Joan Sims*
CHARLOTTE	*Dilys Lay*
ANNIE	*Valerie Carton*
THE VISITOR	*Patrick Cargill*

On the stage is a large gilt frame; the picture within it is unlit and appears as darkness. A lady GUIDE *is showing visitors round.*

GUIDE. Now, ladies and gentlemen, we come to one of the most interesting portraits in the castle. It's the fourth duke and family, done in seventeen-eighty after the manner of Sir Joshua Reynolds. I'm afraid it's hung in rather a bad light . . . I'll just turn the lamp on it.

(She exits and the picture lights up. It is horrific. Represented are the fourth duke, his wife and children, not to mention the family animals, all in front of the Mansion over which the sun is setting.

On the right—stage L—*we have an oak tree under which the* DUCHESS *sits with her baby on her lap. She wears a dull pink dress, a white lace bosom and collar piece, and a black lace shoulder-piece, with a spray of flowers stuck into the bosom. Her hair is in pompadour style, with a long back and a plait intertwined with a pink ribbon wound round the front. Her baby is hideously out of proportion and is much too small. It has a bright pink sash.*

ANNIE, *her daughter, an anaemic child, kneels on the grass in front of her. She has a white dress, with a blue sash; she has lifted her skirt to hold a posy of rather peculiar flowers—not very successfully as quite a few have fallen on the floor. Around her dark hair is a white bandeau, in which she appears to have stuck some heather.*

To the left of her mother is CHARLOTTE, *a fat and repulsive child. She wears a white and blue cavalier-type cockade hat, a pink sash, and a white dress with a rucked-up effect on the skirt. Like her mother and sister she has red buckle shoes.*

She is reaching up towards a repellent dead grouse with spread-wings, held at arm's length by the DUKE. *He wears the kilt, a sporran,*

*

5

cream waistcoat, dark brown cutaway coat, a strange tam o'shanter with a large red cockade, pink and white tartan socks, and brown buckle shoes. He has various accoutrements, including a dirk, and a water bottle on a green cord. Under his right arm is an enormous flintlock sporting gun. This is angled so as to point directly at the ugliest liver-and-white dog in the world. This is curled up at his feet on the grass and has probably been dead for months. Just beside it is a toy cart with three wheels and some more of those strange flowers.

On the left of the picture is a panting gamekeeper resembling Noah. Only the top of him is visible. This wears a green coat, scarlet waist-coat and a very suggestive sporran indeed. The lower half is concealed by two vast greyhounds, each a cross between a Saluki and a Bedlington. These he is endeavouring to keep apart with leather leashes.

On the floor in front of the hounds, the head of a dead stag pro-trudes into the picture. It has a very unhappy look in its one visible eye.

Up L are some fir trees and behind them, the hills and the setting sun.

And, by the way, there's a large grey smudge next to Mother)

DUKE.	The day I revealed to the family
	I'd engaged at enormous expense
	A practically fashionable painter,
	The joy that they felt was immense;
	Well, now was the moment to capture us all
	For delighted posterity's gaze.
	Now we've sat with the dogs
	Through the rain, storm and fogs
	For one hundred and forty-six tedious days . . .
ALL.	Beautiful family portrait,
DUKE.	We have been here for many a day.
DUCHESS.	And at the first sitting
	I just held my knitting
	The Duke's heir was still on the way.
CHARLOTTE.	When we started we also had Grannie
ANNIE.	But we lost her last week from the gout,
DUCHESS.	And this grey smudge you see just behind me
	Is where Grannie's been painted out
	Of our . . .
ALL.	Beautiful family portrait.
DUKE.	We must sit here all night it is true,
CHARLOTTE.	But the mornings are damp,
	And I find I get cramp,
	In the place where I'm touching the dew.
DUKE.	You may wonder at my sad expression
	It's the grouse that is causing me pain,
	For this bird is so horribly high now
	It's about to start flying again.

ANNIE.	The reason these flowers look peculiar Can't be blamed on the artist I vow, They were tulips when he started painting But I fear they're chrysanthemums now.
DUKE.	During June the stag died of starvation,
DUCHESS.	That was when Father started to cough,
ANNIE.	And little dog Tray Got right in the way
CHARLOTTE.	When that bloody great flintlock went off . . .
	In our
ALL.	Beautiful family portrait,
DUKE.	Though the picture is now in good shape, This Jacobite Troupe Is still holding its group Helping Bonnie Prince Charlie escape.
CHARLOTTE.	Miss Macdonald may get all the credit For the true facts will never appear,
DUKE.	He came here disguised as the feminine gender
DUCHESS.	But we soon found out he was just a pretender, So we're carefully hiding our country's defender— Do you want to know where?

BONNIE PRINCE CHARLIE (*emerging from under her skirt*) Och, I'm here!

BLACK-OUT

A LA SARTRE

Performed in *High Spirits*

<table>
<tr><td>*Words by*
David Climie</td><td>*Music by*
John Pritchett</td></tr>
</table>

Characters

GENERAL	*Cyril Ritchard*
ARDÈLE	*Diana Churchill*
JEAN	*Leslie Crowther*
ORPHÉE	*Ian Carmichael*
ELECTRA	*Dilys Lay*
DEATH	*Patrick Cargill*
RIGOR MORTIS	*Thelma Ruby*

The curtain rises on a sleazy French provincial railway station, trying to look as symbolic as possible. Furnish to taste, except there should be a "DAMES" and a "MESSIEURS" door on either side of the stage and an abandoned-looking bed complete with rumpled clothes in the background.

The family are discovered scattered about the stage. THE GENERAL, who is the father, ARDÈLE, his wife, and JEAN, the son, are all dressed in vaguely Edwardian clothes—the GENERAL in uniform if possible. ELECTRA, the daughter, wears a ballet skirt and polo-neck jersey. They sing in hopeless tones, although ELECTRA is a little brighter than the rest. She must give an impression of remaining fresh and unspoiled by the general air of decay throughout.

ALL. Sprigs of French aristocracy—
ELECTRA. Un—
JEAN.   Deux—
GENERAL.   Trois—
ARDÈLE.   Quatre!
JEAN. Not in the least bit concerned with democracy—
ELECTRA. Something left over from Jean Paul Sartre.
ARDÈLE. For this station's our own private hell we'd explain
      Dreamed up by the boys back in old Saint Germaine;
GENERAL. And to make it more hellish, we've music and songs
      In a play where we're certain no music belongs.

    ARDÈLE (*moaning loudly*) Aiiieee! Why must we live on a station? We are of the nobility, General dear.
    GENERAL. Decadence and decay, Ardèle.
    JEAN. Once we lived at the Gare de Lyons.

8

ELECTRA. *I* prefer this little station.

GENERAL. Ah yes, Electra—c'est magnifique, mais ce n'est pas la Gare.

JEAN. Why must our lives be set on a permanent way?

ARDÈLE. Now, Jean—we must not despise the station in life to which it has pleased Monsieur Anouilh to call us.

ALL.   We're four Existential characters—

JEAN *and* ELECTRA.

      Strange ones—

ARDÈLE. Maman—

GENERAL.   Et Papa.

JEAN.   I'm young and treacherous—

GENERAL. I'm old and lecherous;

ARDÈLE. I'm more than slightly gaga.

ALL.   We'll sit right here till hell freezes and

      All be as happy as pigs.

      All doomed to horrible thoughts and diseases

ELECTRA (*indicating Ardèle's red wig*)

      And even more horrible wigs.

ARDÈLE. I'm a motherly tart

      By M'sieu Jean Paul Sartre;

GENERAL. I'm a filthy old father by Camus;

JEAN.   I'm a decadent heel

      From the pen of Anouilh,

ELECTRA. And I am the cat's pyjamas!

ALL.   Tra-la-la-la, tra-la-la-la, Woe! Lackaday!

      Toujours de douleur and jamais de gai;

      We've nothing to live for but plenty to say

      In an Existential musical play.

  (*There is a terrible agonized squawk off stage*)

ARDÈLE. That is the cry of the wombat—in combat.

GENERAL. No, Ardèle—that was my poor frustrated sister, who is suffering from a terrible affliction——

  (*Everyone moans*)

—hiccups! We never speak of her in the family.

JEAN. We never speak of Aunt Antigone, Aunt Colombe and Aunt Euridice either—they who live together in the buffet.

ARDÈLE (*pawing Jean*) Those three old ladies locked in depravity.

GENERAL. Leave the boy alone, Ardèle.

ELECTRA (*sidling round Jean*) But, Father—he *is* handsome.

(*Singing*)   Frère Jean—tu es bon

        Dormez-vous—avec who?

JEAN (*singing*)   Une amie ce soir, dear;
                          I share her with papa, dear.

GENERAL (*singing*)   Oui, c'est bien!

ARDÈLE (*singing*)   Oui, c'est bien!

(JEAN *goes moodily into the* "MESSIEURS" *ignoring* ARDÈLE'S *pleading hand.* ELECTRA *dances across the stage in front of the other two*)

GENERAL (*restraining her*) Electra—fresh young innocence is one thing—stealing the limelight is another.

ARDÈLE. To think our daughter would turn out to be

(*She sings*)   Au clair de la Bloom-eur . . .

ELECTRA (*singing*)   Mon ami Cocteau!
                          Have you heard the rumeur?
                          Jean Marais must go.

(ARDÈLE *moans loudly*)

GENERAL (*singing*)   Ardèle—what can the matter be?
ARDÈLE (*indicating the* "MESSIEURS")
                          Jean—he's so long à l'affaire!

(*The mysterious* STRANGER *enters in a trench coat and slouch hat*)

STRANGER (*singing*)   Ring around the tomb, boys—
                          Death in the Living Room boys.
                          Portman! Tutin! All fall down!

ELECTRA. Death? But I do not want death. I want love! Love! When will it come? When?

GENERAL. We each of us live in a box, Electra. You must wait until love enters *your* little box—whatever I mean.

ARDÈLE (*to the Stranger*) My friend—I think I shall fall in love with you.

STRANGER. Would you fall in love with Death?

ARDÈLE. Why not? Everyone else around here does. Oh, take me away from all this—I know where we could make beautiful music together. (*She sings*)

> Come for a roll in the gutter
> In the new uninhibited way;
> I remember I knew a
> Most charming old sewer;
> So why don't we go there and play?
> And I know a convenient quagmire
> Where the mud is both vintage and free.
> So follow, friends, follow!
> Let's all go and wallow
> And roll in the gutter with me—he-he—
> Roll in the gutter with me!

(*The* STRANGER *picks up* ARDÈLE *and is about to make off with her when the* GENERAL *stops him*)

GENERAL. Stop! Before you take her away, I think you should know that my wife—she will confess it herself—was formerly a woman of the streets practising under the name of Charlotte Russe.

(*The* STRANGER *drops* ARDÈLE *on the bed*)

STRANGER. Ah—an open tart!
ARDÈLE. Now everything is spoiled—everything is ruined.
ELECTRA. When will love rise out of this mud? When?

(ORPHÉE *enters. He wears a zip jacket, and a cap over one eye. He carries a sledgehammer. He walks as though dancing*)

ORPHÉE (*walking straight up to Electra*) My name is Orphée. I love you.
ELECTRA. And I love you, Orphée.
GENERAL. Tchah! He's just a Jean-Louis Barrault-boy! All this talk of love makes me sick!

(*Singing*) I'll sing you a song that is merry and fresh,
    Concerning the sordid desires of the flesh—
    Lust! Lust! Lust!
    It's an existential must!
    Don't mind the billing and don't mind the cooing;
    Come on, young man—you must be up and doing
    With lust! Lust! Lust!
    Though you may feel a certain disgust,
    Don't be refined with it
    Just soak your mind in it—
    Lust, beautiful Lust!

(*To Electra*) There—what d'you think of that?
ELECTRA. It's no good, Father. You cannot soil our love with your decadence. I shall remain untouched.
GENERAL (*to Orphée*) You're in for a very dull marriage, young man.
ELECTRA. The evil shadow of this family shall not come between us. Orphée—do you love me?
ORPHÉE. I love you.
ELECTRA. With a pure and simple spiritual love, transcending mere physical desire?
ORPHÉE. Of course.
ELECTRA (*yelling*) Then why don't you hit me with that sledge-hammer?

(*Singing*)	Oh, a poke in the eye from a wonderful guy Has replaced all that old lovey-dove. So snatch me—grab me—shoot me—stab me— Kill me—this is love!

ORPHÉE (*singing*)	Oh, a sock on the jaw from the girl I adore Would transport me to Heaven above. So slug me—slosh me—kick me—cosh me— Kill me—this is love!

ELECTRA.	And as you stand before me—I've one thing to beg; Just to prove that you adore me—baby, bite my leg!

ORPHÉE ⎫
ELECTRA ⎬ (*together*) ⎰ Oh, a love that rough-houses delights the Keith Prowses;
       ⎱ Let's neck with that old boxing glove.

ELECTRA. Skip the kisses, Buster—get the knuckle-duster.

ORPHÉE ⎫
ELECTRA ⎭ (*together*) Kill me—this is love!

(*They both knock each other flat*)

GENERAL. Sometimes I feel a little out of touch with our children.

STRANGER (*advancing on the lovers*) You are happy now but your love cannot last. I can offer you eternal bliss. Why not let me push you under the next train?

ORPHÉE. Would you really do that for us?

STRANGER. Oh, yes. Maybe I'm a sentimental old fool but I like to see the young people happy.

ARDÈLE. Perhaps you could do it for all of us?

GENERAL. Now, Ardèle—we mustn't impose on the gentleman.

STRANGER. Oh, I think I could take care of you all. If you'd just line up along the edge of the platform—*all* of you!

(JEAN *enters from the* "MESSIEURS" *with a chain round his neck in a noose. They all line up along the footlights and stare into the audience*)

GENERAL. Of course, it's a pity there aren't any trains on this line.

ALL (*singing*)	Existentional!
	We know it's not conventional,
	Or three-dimensional,
	But that's intentional!
	And really we don't give a cuss;
	For we've all got futility,
	All got futility,
	All got futility plus!

ARDÈLE (*reciting*)	Remember those dear old-timers?
	Mauriac, Genet and Sartre?
	Those are the boys who begrime us—
	Those are the boys without heart.
	Never mind Ethel M. Dell, lads,
	Anouilh faced without fear
	The fact that society's hell, lads!
	Yeah—he had it *here*!
	(*She indicates the pit of the stomach*)

ALL (*singing*)	Futility!
	We think that life is just utility,
	Without virility,
	Or amiability,
	And really that's O.K. by us—
	For though we're intellectual,
	We're ineffectual—
	We're ineffectual . . .

(*A "Keep-Death-off-the-Roads"* WIDOW *enters*)

WIDOW. I'm Rigor Mortis—may I set in?

ALL (*singing*)	We're ineffectual plus!

CURTAIN

MR HENDERSON

Performed in *High Spirits*

Lyric by
Peter Myers & Alec Grahame

Music by
John Pritchett

HAT CHECK GIRL

Diana Churchill

A HAT CHECK GIRL *is discovered.*

It was two a.m. at the *Blue Parrot Club.*
I was tired—I was dead on my feet,
Then he walked in and gave me his coat
And my heart seemed to miss a beat.
I checked his hat
That was usually that,
Then he said, "Can I walk home with you?"
Of course when a customer starts to get fresh
I usually know what to do . . .

But . . .

There was something about Mr Henderson
You know the feeling I guess,
I'm a girl who knows all of the answers
But he made me feel like a princess.
Now a check girl gets plenty of chances
And I'd heard the whole routine before,
There was something about Mr Henderson
That I thought was worth waiting for.

We took a little apartment
Way up on the seventh floor,
We hadn't much money but I did my best
And I couldn't have asked for more.
We were happy alone
Up there on our own
Just we two in our little flat,
I figured some day we'd get married
But we just didn't get round to that.

Still . . .

There was something about Mr Henderson,
Soon his career reached the heights
And he knew, oh, such elegant people
That we dared not be seen out at nights.

14

So I guess that I just didn't blame him
When he told me one day we were through,
There was something about Mr Henderson
If he said it was best—well, he knew.

Now it's two a.m. at the *Blue Parrot Club*
And I'm back where I started again,
But those years have made quite a difference
And I don't have much trouble with men.
This evening he came,
He looked just the same
And he smiled the same smile I had known,
There was nothing about him changed one little bit
Except that he wasn't alone.

And . . .

There was something about Mrs Henderson
That seemed familiar to me,
I had somehow the feeling I knew her
Though she wasn't my sort I could see,
Then I glanced at us both in a mirror
And I realized why I felt so,
There was something about Mrs Henderson
She looked like me—ten years ago.
Mr Henderson, you were nice—to know . . .

BLACK AND WHITE WIDOW

Performed in *Intimacy at Eight*

Lyric by
Peter Myers & Alec Grahame

Music by
Ronald Cass

GIRL   *Eunice Gayson*

A lovely GIRL *is discovered sitting on a high stool at a bar.*

I sit all alone in a cocktail bar
A theatre, a night club or some cinema,
Unheeded
Un-needed.
My man lets me roam,
My man is my husband and he stays at home. . . .

I'm a television widow and I hate it,
I'm a television widow—help me Lord,
He stays home by a cosy fire enjoying himself
While I have to go out and get bored.

I'm a victim of video and I loathe it,
I keep longing for the love that once was mine,
What has this thing got that I haven't got?
I keep asking myself "What's its Line?"

I had nothing to say at each Sunday night play,
But the Thursday repeat was too cruel,
And I will not lose face and take second place
To his orgies with Muffin the Mule.

Each anniversary he used to bring me posies,
Now he brings Queen Alexandra Palace Roses,
Oh, to be a merry widow may be all very well
But to be a tele widow is just plain merry Hell!

He sits and he leers as Miss Peters appears
Though he says it isn't intentional,
But what will he do when my nightmare comes true
On the day television gets three-dimensional?

There's some teleview divorcing in the offing,
When they've heard my tale the court will not be scoffing,
The chambermaid will testify she'll never forget
The man who spent the night at Brighton with a T.V. set.

16

I'VE BEEN FRAMED

Performed in *Intimacy at Eight*

Lyric by
David Climie

Music by
Ronald Cass

MODEL   *Joan Sims*

The curtain rises on an artist's MODEL *posed on a dais.*

MODEL. Sir Alfred—can I rest now? . . . Thank you, Sir Alfred. (*She relaxes and sits on a chair*)

I've sat for every artist back to eighteen-seventy-five;
They've immortalized me time and time again;
I've posed in every posture you could possibly contrive,
And one or two I couldn't quite explain.
I met the pre-Raphaelites but passed some rather gayer nights
With all the post-impressionistic group;
And I really got pally with that lovely Mr Dali
Who saw me as a fur-lined bowl of soup.
I've been painted, I've been sketched—I've been carved and I've
    been etched,
And, although I'm just a little past my prime,
Every painting to be classy must incorporate my chassis—
Oh, the canvas that I've covered in my time!

There was Monet, there was Manet, there was Masson and
    Matisse,
There was Dégas, there was Dufy, there was Dick;
And the one who did the bust of me in bits of candle grease,
And entitled it "The Lady with the Wick".
I simply cannot tell you all the movements I've been through;
Now, if anyone complains, I simply drawl:
"If it's good enough for Gainsborough, it's good enough for you;
I'm the oldest artist's model of them all!"

There was Turner, there was Tissot, there was jellied eels and gin;
There was Sargent, Sickert, sandwiches and stout;
If I drew a bath, then Mr Dégas drew me getting in,
(Mr Renoir always drew me getting out).
I remember once, in Paris, posing barefoot—to the neck—
Which precipitated quite a vulgar brawl,
So I told the artist "Your behaviour's much *too* loose, Lautrec,
For the oldest artist's model of them all."

17

They used to give me paintings when they couldn't pay my fee,
And I've got them stacked at home on every shelf;
I've got fourteen by Derain hung around my *salle de bain,*
And Modigliani in the *bain* itself.

I've got portraits done by Vuillard, Vivin, Vlaminck and
        Vermeer,
By Burra and by Berard and by Blake;
I remember asking Van Gogh what had happened to his ear,
And he struck me—with a tube of crimson lake.
I often sit and wonder just exactly *how* I look;
Am I cubist or surrealist, short or tall?
I sometimes wish I had the time to have a photo took
Of the oldest artist's model of them all. . . .

(*Spoken*) I'm ready now, Sir Alfred. . . . What position do you
want, Sir Alfred?. . . . Oh, Sir Alfred! What—and miss the
television?

BLACK-OUT

STUDENT SONG

Performed in *Intimacy at Eight*

Words by
Peter Myers & Alec Grahame

Music by
John Pritchett

Characters

DRAMA STUDENT   *Joan Sims*
MEDICAL STUDENT   *Ron Moody*
ART STUDENT   *Dilys Lay*

A romantic group in silhouette is discovered.

ALL.
Students' life was so romantic
In the days of yesteryear,
When Heidelburg
Was an idle burg
Except for duels and drinking beer.
Now life isn't so romantic,
We are quite a different type,
We persevere
Training for a career.

(*The lights come up revealing typical students: a* MEDICAL
STUDENT, *in a dirty sports coat and flannels with a pipe; an* ART
STUDENT, *in dirndl skirt and blouse and with appalling costume
jewellery; and a* DRAMA STUDENT, *in slacks, sweater and dark
glasses*)

ART STUDENT. With dirndl—
DRAMA STUDENT.   Sunglasses—
MEDICAL STUDENT.   And pipe . . .
ALL. Forward students of Britain,
MEDICAL STUDENT. Medicine
DRAMA STUDENT.   Drama
ART STUDENT.   And Arts.
DRAMA STUDENT. I stand out in a crowd
For I talk very loud,
MEDICAL STUDENT. And I chase the nurses at Barts.
ART STUDENT. You may think I'm a fake,
But to me life's opaque,
For when I look at Epstein I bleed.
DRAMA STUDENT. I talk for hours on worse than death but
haven't yet been fated.

19

MEDICAL STUDENT. I can't remember all the dates on which I've
                   operated,
ART STUDENT.   My soulmate's name is Evan and it's all been
                   sublimated,
ALL.   Students of the modern breed!

ART STUDENT.   I got this blouse from C & A but you would
                   never think it,
                  I've completely changed its message now
                   with my barbaric trinket,
                  Dympna and I share a flat in the one un-
                   fashionable mews in town,
                  We've achieved a new shape in Regency
                   Stripe—because ours goes across not
                   down,
                  I only see films at a Classic house, never ever
                   the Regal or Rex
                  And I was laid waste by Mr Magoo—how
                   he engenders *Sex*!

MEDICAL STUDENT. I'm inheriting Dad's practice so he's sent me
                   here to make perfect,
                  I talk about gall stones all through lunch
                   until you've had a surfeit.
                  What a sense of humour—doctored drinks at
                   my parties are the rule!
                  Oh, the witty thing I did with that corpse I
                   pinched from the Medical School,
                  I get dexadrines and other drugs to aid my
                   friends' desires,
                  I've an endless supply of bedpans—and I put
                   them all on spires.

DRAMA STUDENT.   I always knew that to go on the stage was
                   really my career
                  Ever since I appeared at my Convent School
                   in the title part—King Lear.
                  I know I'm better than Claire Bloom—
                   dialects, English and foreign,
                  Peut-être I'm not ready for St Joan—but *Mon
                   Dieu*, my Mrs Warren!
                  At RADA we lead *La Vie Bohème* and I once
                   did a thing bizarre—
                  I had supper with Naomi Jacob, and actu-
                   ally smoked a cigar!
ALL.   Forward, students of Britain.
MEDICAL STUDENT. Medicine
DRAMA STUDENT.   Drama

ART STUDENT.	And Arts.
MEDICAL STUDENT.	I never talk tripe I just stuff my pipe
GIRLS.	And we're intellectual tarts.
ALL.	We are sure you'll agree That you see in we three The types who are bound to succeed.
ART STUDENT.	You can dodge *me* at the Arts Ball—in the tableaux I'm an elf.
DRAMA STUDENT.	As the lead in Scunthorpe Repertory you *may* deny *me* wealth.
MEDICAL STUDENT.	But you'll find you *have* to take *me*—I come under National Health.
ALL.	Students of the modern—
ART STUDENT.	Stark
DRAMA STUDENT.	Stiff
MEDICAL STUDENT.	And sodden—
ALL.	Students of the modern breed.

CURTAIN

HOLIDAY QUEEN

Performed in *Intimacy at Eight*

Lyric by
Peter Myers & Alec Grahame

Music by
Norman Dannatt

Miss Potting Hill

Joan Sims

Miss Potting Hill, *a beauty queen, is discovered self-consciously holding a trophy cup.*

At Potting Hill West Garden Suburb
They've crowned me the holiday queen.
Oh, the things that they did when they chose me
Right in front of the Odeon screen.
Everything I treasured
Was examined and then measured
With the organ playing *Love Will Find a Way.*
All the other girls seemed far more glamorous than me
But I got picked because they said I won on points, you see.
And got a kiss from Maxwell Reed—that's how I bruised my
    knee
Oh, the life of a holiday queen is ever so gay.

The Potting Hill Chamber of Commerce
Made my moment of triumph complete,
Arrayed on a float with some flowers and a goat,
I was ready to go on the street.
To start the parade
Came the Boys' Brigade
With a tableau called "Fairies at Play".
Then came Britain's new Home Guard camouflaged with leafy
    boughs,
Then the Co-op dairy girls with a banner "Perfect Cows"
And a housewives' demonstration—"How to satisfy your
    Spouse"—
Oh, the life of a holiday queen is ever so gay.

The Potting Hill Mayor and Council
Gave me prizes—a whole ton of Tide,
And a beautiful holiday wardrobe—
The best Marks and Spencer provide.
The men all guessed my weight
At the British Legion Fête
A fête worse than death I should say.

I paid a royal visit to the International Ballet
As reward I got the freedom of the local Mecca Palais
And a lovely week-end with my friend at Butlin's—in a chalet.
Oh, the life of a holiday queen is ever so gay.

My message to British womanhood is always do your best,
You'll find that you come out on top if you just stick out your
    chest,
And in a strapless bathing suit you must tuck down your vest,
Oh, the life of a holiday queen is ever so gay.

BLACK-OUT

CASE HISTORY

Performed in *The Irving Revue*

Lyric by
Peter Myers & Alec Grahame

Music by
John Pritchett

NURSE   Eunice Gayson

A NURSE is discovered in an empty private ward.

A fading bunch of flowers, the last of the grapes,
Now I have to tidy up the room.
I open up the windows and make up the bed,
There's another patient coming soon.
But I'll remember, if I may,
The one that left yesterday . . .

The patient came two months ago,
He was quiet and very polite,
And this time the strangest thing happened,
It was I who could not sleep at night.
I was used to the old situation,
Patients usually fall for their nurse,
But right from the start
I knew in my heart
It had happened this time in reverse.

Think about the routine, think about my work,
Think about my summer spell of leave,
Think about anything to make me forget
The heart upon my over-starched sleeve.
But whenever I'm in here
The past will seem much too near . . .

The patient did so very well
The new patient in private ward C.
I know a nurse mustn't show feeling
But it wasn't so easy for me,
He was so uncomplaining and grateful,
But I had to confess I could see
That shy sort of smile,
That made life worth while
Wasn't given especially to me.

Time to change the name on the door of the room,
Time to change the card upon the chart,
Time to change the pillow and time to change the clothes,
And time to have a change of heart.
Easy though it seems to do—
Not when it happens to you . . .

The patient left here yesterday,
But I found all my dreams had come true
The last time that we were together.
Yes—he told me that he loved me too.
All I have is that one perfect moment
To remember the whole of my life.
For his personal things,
His keys and his rings,
Must be sent to the late patient's wife.

CURTAIN

SCANDAL ON THE SABBATH

Performed in *Ad Lib*

Lyric by	*Music by*
Peter Myers & Alec Grahame	Norman Dannatt
SCOTS GIRL	*Daphne Anderson*

A young Scots girl is discovered.

We are not allowed to mention Maria Lynne
Since the day she took the silken road to sin,
But we don't mind telling you what we heard
If you'll cross your heart that you won't say a word . . .

She washed out an undie on Sunday
And hung it to dry in the sun,
When everyone knows that a Monday
Is the day when such things should be done.
She knew it was wrong on the Sabbath
To reveal how a girl is costumed
But she washed out an undie on Sunday
So we know that Maria is doomed.

She washed out an undie on Sunday,
A fragment of lace and silk blue
Was fluttering there on her clothes line
And it wasn't a petticoat too.
When the minister saw it a-blowing
A blush on his worthy cheek bloomed,
And he hurriedly went to the vestry
So we know that Maria is doomed.

She washed out an undie on Sunday,
Ignoring the powers divine,
Who to punish her strengthened the West wind
And blew it away from her line.
And a visiting millionaire banker
Was enveloped in silk so perfumed
That we thought he would swoon for a moment
So we know that Maria is doomed.

He picked up that undie on Sunday
And the story cannot be denied.
When he very politely returned it
The brazen girl asked him inside.
He married her yesterday morning
And we feel we must blush for her shame
For she washed out an undie on Sunday—
Next Sunday I'm doing the same!

APARTMENT WITH FEAR

By Peter Myers & Lionel Harris

Performed in *In Tempo*

Characters

HOUSE AGENT	A BODY
MAN	A BUTLER
WOMAN	A HEADLESS CHILD
A GHOST	A MONSTER

The HOUSE AGENT *is discovered spotlighted in front of the curtains.*

HOUSE AGENT (*into the telephone*) Hullo . . . Is that Mr Jones? Are you still looking for a flat? I think I have just the place for you. I've made an appointment for you at two . . . No, No. Two in the morning.

BLACK-OUT

(*The curtains open on a sinister apartment. It is in a terrible condition, the paper peeling off the wall. There are five doors: the two in the back wall are cupboards and there is a large window between them. In the* L *wall is the front door and a subsidiary door. There is another door in the* R *wall. A* WOMAN, *dressed as in Charles Addams' cartoons, is standing down* L. *There is a knocking at the front door. Without saying a word she beckons. The front door opens by itself, revealing the* MAN, *rather timorous*)

MAN. Er—excuse me. But is this flat thirteen?

WOMAN. Yes. (*With shrill eerie laughter*) He said you were coming. (*She gives another laugh*)

MAN (*entering with some trepidation*) Er—it's a little dark in here.

WOMAN. Yes. Have you a shilling for the meter?

(*She reaches out and takes a coin from his hand. He looks horrified—he hadn't got a coin*)

Thank you.

(*She throws it out of the window. There is a lightning flash*)

That's better.

MAN. Now tell me—is it a very large flat?

WOMAN. Three rooms—(*producing a flagon marked Sulphuric Acid* and a bath. By the way, can I offer you a drink?

MAN (*looking at the flagon*) No, thank you. By the way, are there any conditions attached to the lease?

27

WOMAN. We'll expect you to take the furniture, of course.

MAN. Furniture?

WOMAN. The rack, the thumb-screws and the bedroom suite. You don't object to twin coffins, I hope?

MAN. Er . . .

WOMAN. And of course there'll be a small deposit on the skeleton key.

(*At that moment a gibbering figure in a sheet runs across the set*)

You don't object to spirits, I hope?

MAN. I thought they only came out at midnight.

WOMAN. Yes, but we got an extension to two a.m.

(*A squeaking is heard off stage*)

Oh excuse me, I forgot to put the bat out.

(*She exits through the door down* L. *He glances round and then looks after her through the keyhole of the door. Almost immediately she comes back through the door on the other side of the stage, walks up behind him and gives one of her piercing laughs. He nearly jumps out of his skin*)

MAN. Er—is the lease in your name or your husband's?

WOMAN. My husband and I quarrelled and he left me.

MAN. Oh, I'm sorry to hear that.

WOMAN. Don't distress yourself—he's still very near to me.

(*The* MAN *opens one of the cupboard doors, disclosing a* BODY *with a large knife stuck in it*)

Poor Henry! I always used to tell him, "Comb your moustache".

(*The* BODY *obediently does so. The little* MAN *closes the door hastily*)

And now look from the window. Is it not an entrancing view?

MAN. Well—er . . .

WOMAN. Such a very pretty cemetery. It's so nice being near one's friends. I know you won't be lonely here, they're always dropping in.

(*The sinister* BUTLER *alights on the window-sill with a thud*)

My butler! My dear, *another* young man from the Agents.

(*The* BUTLER, *without a word, pulls out a large knife and fork and sharpens them*)

Not yet, dear. After all, he may take the flat.

MAN. Is it a long lease?

WOMAN. Well, when we took it there was nine hundred and ninety-nine years. There's still seventy-two to go.

(*The* BUTLER, *who has been circling the Man eyeing him, at this point prods him tentatively with the knife*)

MAN. Yeoww!

WOMAN. Don't be so anxious, dear. Go and feed the werewolf or something. There's a fresh corpse in the icebox.

(*The* BUTLER *exits* L)

MAN. Why are you giving up the flat?

WOMAN. Well, we would have moved before, only—(*she opens the other cupboard door, revealing an Egyptian relic*) Mummy was so comfortable here.

(*A* HEADLESS CHILD *enters*)

Ah, my little dead-end kid. Have you washed your face?

(*The* CHILD *produces its head from behind its back*)

You've missed behind the ears again. Darling, would you like to sleep with your friend tonight?

(*The* CHILD *signifies assent*)

Then off you go. (*She hands him a large spade*) He's at St Paul's.

(*The* CHILD *exits*)

MAN. I understand your wanting to move. Children are so difficult in a flat.

WOMAN. Yes. Little footmarks everywhere. (*She points at the ceiling*)

(*Frankenstein's* MONSTER *enters, marches right across the set and out*)

(*In ecstasy*) Frankieeeee!

(*At this moment the* BUTLER *enters with a large meat-axe*)

Patience, dear. (*To the Man*) I'm afraid my butler's getting hungry. If you won't take the flat, you'll stay to dinner, won't you?

MAN. Well, it's not a bad proposition. Electric lighting——

(*Another lightning flash*)

—running water——

(*A drip falls on him from the ceiling*)

—and every ancient convenience . . . But *no*!

WOMAN⎫
BUTLER⎭(*together ; menacing him*) Why not?

MAN. *I just can't stand your bloody wallpaper!*

BLACK-OUT